Sports-Graphics

Shape of the Game

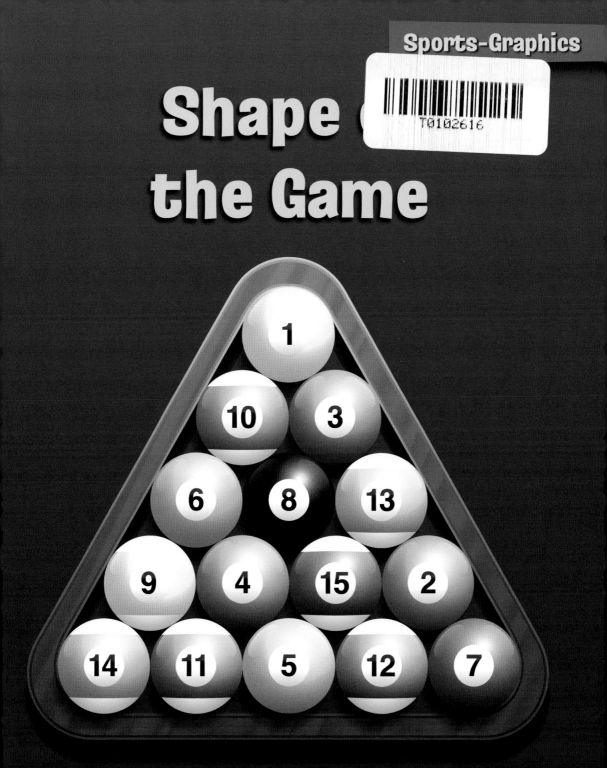

Heather DiLorenzo Williams

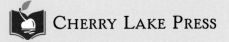

CHERRY LAKE PRESS

Published in the United States of America by Cherry Lake Publishing Group
Ann Arbor, Michigan
www.cherrylakepublishing.com

Reading Adviser: Beth Walker Gambro, MS, Ed., Reading Consultant, Yorkville, IL

Photo Credits: cover: ©Praewpalilin / Getty Images; ©bortonia / Getty Images; ©elinedesignservices / Getty Images; ©Rvector / Shutterstock; page 5: ©Jessica Orozco, page 5: ©XonkArts / Getty Images; page 5: ©EgudinKa / Getty Images; page 7: ©Jessica Orozco; page 7: ©Roman Prysiazhniuk / Getty Images; page 8: ©Jessica Orozco; page 9: ©Jessica Orozco / ; page 10: ©Jessica Orozco; page 11: ©Jessica Orozco; page 13: ©Jessica Orozco / ; page 14: ©Jessica Orozco; page 15: ©stevezmina1 / Getty Images; page 16: ©biolalabet / Shutterstock; page 16: ©Brovko Serhii / Shutterstock; page 16: ©Jessica Orozco; page 17: ©andrewvect / Shutterstock; page 17: ©aurielaki / Shutterstock; page 19: ©Jessica Orozco; page 20: ©GoodStudio / Shutterstock; page 20: ©Top Vector Studio / Shutterstock; page 20: ©Paragorn Dangsombroon / Shutterstock; page 20: ©JuliarStudio / Getty Images; page 21: ©Pretty Vectors / Shutterstock; page 21: ©freehandz / Getty Images; page 22: ©Jessica Orozco page 23: ©DoggieMonkey / Getty Images; page 23: ©apagafonova / Getty Images; page 23: ©Ihor Reshetniak / Getty Images; page 23: ©FishDesigns / Getty Images; page 25: ©SofiaV / Shutterstock; page 26: ©Jessica Orozco; page 26: ©Gianni Ferrari / Contributor / Getty Images; page 28: ©grimgram / Getty Images; page 28: ©Belliely / Getty Images; page 29: ©kup1984 / Getty Images; page 29: ©djvstock / Getty Images

Cherry Lake Press is an imprint of Cherry Lake Publishing Group.

Library of Congress Cataloging-in-Publication Data
Library of Congress Cataloging-in-Publication Data has been filed and is available at catalog.loc.gov.

Cherry Lake Publishing Group would like to acknowledge the work of the Partnership for 21st Century Learning, a Network of Battelle for Kids. Please visit *http://www.battelleforkids.org/networks/p21* for more information.

Printed in the United States of America

Note from publisher: Websites change regularly, and their future contents are outside of our control. Supervise children when conducting any recommended online searches for extended learning opportunities.

Heather DiLorenzo Williams is a former English teacher and school librarian. She has a passion for seeing readers of all ages connect with others through stories and experiences. Heather has written more than 50 books for children. She enjoys walking her dog, reading, and watching sports. She lives in North Carolina with her husband and two children.

CONTENTS

Shapes in Sports

Athletes need rules when they play sports. Rules make the game fair. Some rules are about the area of the field or court. Some are about the equipment used. That's where shapes come in handy. If some basketball teams practiced on a 30 x 30 foot (9 x 9 meter) square, and some teams practiced on a 70 x 50 foot (21 x 15 m) rectangle, games between them would not be evenly matched. This is why sports rules cover shapes and dimensions. All basketball games are played on a rectangle-shaped court. Courts are the same size for each age group. Other sports have similar rules. This gives teams an equal playing field.

Basic Sports Shapes

SPHERE

A sphere is round and solid. This shape has no edges.

RHOMBUS

A rhombus is a four-sided shape. It has four equal, straight sides. The angles of opposite corners are the same.

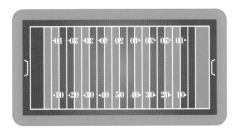

RECTANGLE

A rectangle is a four-sided shape. It has four right angles. Opposite sides are equal in length and parallel. (Squares are both rectangles *and* rhombuses.)

TRIANGLE

A triangle is a three-sided shape. Its angles add up to 180 degrees.

CHAPTER 1

Multi-Sport Dimensions

Most goal sports take place on a rectangle. Goal sports include basketball, football, and soccer. The goal is the focus of the game. This is how teams score. There is a goal on each end of the field or court. Courts and fields are longer on the sides. They have four equal corners. They are all 90-degree angles. Having goals on the short ends makes scoring and defending the goals easier. This would not be possible with a square playing area. Players might not have as much room to spread out. Straight lines and corners also create clear boundaries.

Court Dimensions

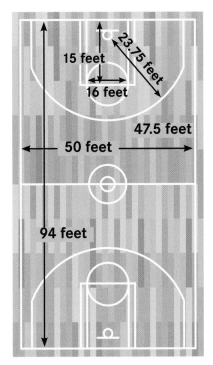

BASKETBALL COURTS

- National Basketball Association (NBA), Women's National Basketball Association (WNBA), and National Collegiate Athletic Association (NCAA) basketball courts are the same size. They measure 94 feet x 50 feet (29 x 15 m).

- High school basketball courts are 84 x 50 feet (26 x 15 m).

- Middle school courts are 74 x 42 feet (23 x 13 m).

TENNIS COURTS

- All tennis courts are the same size. Level and player age don't matter.

- In a doubles tennis match, players have an extra 4.5 feet (1.4 m) on each side of the court. In a singles match, this area is out of bounds.

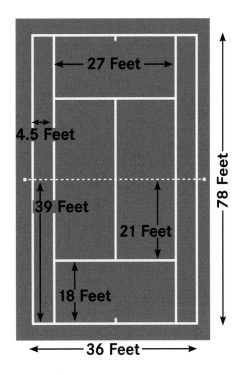

Soccer Pitch Shapes

Soccer fields are different sizes. It depends on the age of the players and the number of people on each team. Youth soccer fields are smaller than professional fields. Those can be anywhere from 100 to 130 yards (91 to 119 m) long and 50 to 100 yards (46 to 91 m) wide.

FIELD A:
YOUTH
4 AGAINST 4

FIELD B:
YOUTH
7 AGAINST 7

FIELD C:
YOUTH
9 AGAINST 9

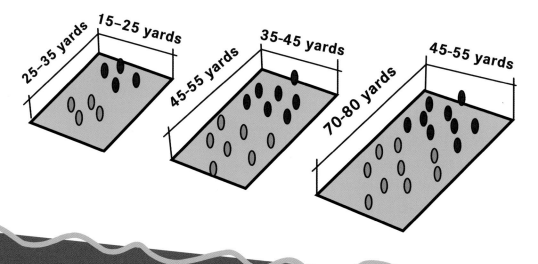

FAST FACTS

Modern soccer was invented in England in the 1800s, many years before the metric system was created. Soccer fields were measured using yards instead of meters. Today, even in countries where the metric system is used, soccer rules still use the imperial system.

Shapes in Pool

Pool is made up of many shapes. These include a rectangular table, spherical balls, and a triangular rack.

TABLE
Shape: Rectangle
Dimensions: 59 x 103 inches
(150 x 262 centimeters)

PLAYING SURFACE
Shape: Rectangle
Dimensions: 44 x 88 inches
(112 x 224 cm)

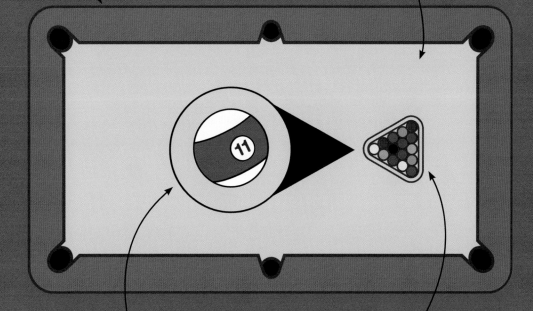

BALLS
Shape: Sphere
Diameter: 2.25 inches
(5.72 cm)

RACK (EIGHT-BALLS)
Shape: Triangle
Dimensions: 10 x 11.25 inches
(25 x 29 cm)

The Baseball Field

A polygon is a shape with three or more sides. How many polygons are on a baseball field?

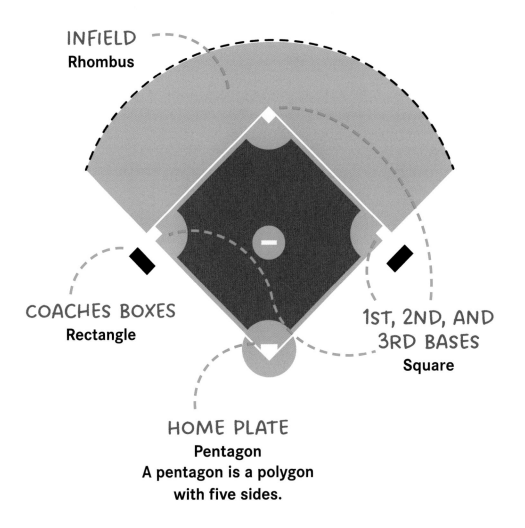

INFIELD
Rhombus

COACHES BOXES
Rectangle

1ST, 2ND, AND
3RD BASES
Square

HOME PLATE
Pentagon
A pentagon is a polygon
with five sides.

Cricket

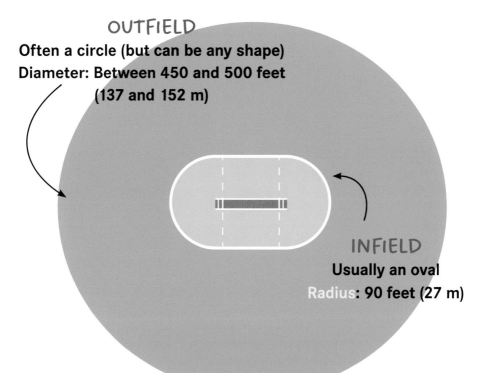

OUTFIELD
**Often a circle (but can be any shape)
Diameter: Between 450 and 500 feet
(137 and 152 m)**

INFIELD
**Usually an oval
Radius: 90 feet (27 m)**

Total Area: Between 159,043 and 196,350 feet (48,476 and 59,847 m)

FAST FACTS

- Cricket uses a bat and a ball, but players . . . bowl.
- Cricket grounds come in many sizes.
- The outfield is usually a circle, but not always! It can be any shape.
- Many professional cricket grounds are the shape of whatever space is available to house them.

CHAPTER 2

Gametime Geometry

Area is how long and how wide a shape is. But some shapes in sports are three-dimensional. Swimming pools are one example. The pool is filled with water. It takes up space in all directions. Rules in swimming determine the length and width of the pool. They also cover depth. Hockey games take place on a flat surface. It looks a lot like a basketball court. But hockey is played on ice. The ice must have a certain thickness to support the players.

Some sports have unusual shapes. Football and hockey are not played with spheres. Some sports equipment comes in a cylinder shape. But each shape has a special purpose.

The Olympic Swimming Pool

Most Olympic swimming events take place in a 10-lane 50-meter pool. Ten swimmers can compete at one time. The minimum depth of these pools is 6 feet, 7 inches, or 6.58 feet (2 m).

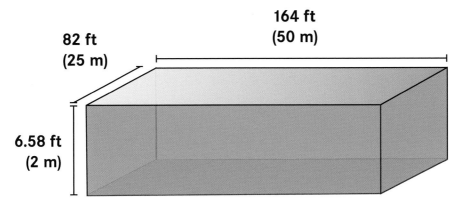

82 ft (25 m)

164 ft (50 m)

6.58 ft (2 m)

To calculate the volume of a 10-lane Olympic pool, first multiply the length times the width times the depth:

length x width x depth = cubic feet

164 FEET X 82 FEET X 6.58 FEET = 88,487.84 CUBIC FEET

Then multiply your total by 7.5. This is because there are 7.5 gallons per cubic foot in a swimming pool.

cubic feet x 7.5 = gallons

88,487.84 X 7.5 = 663,658.8 GALLONS

If the pool is deeper than 6 feet, 7 inches, the volume is greater. An 8-feet deep pool would have a volume of 806,880 gallons:

164 x 82 x 8 = 107,584 cubic feet

107,584 x 7.5 = 806,880 gallons

The Ice Is Right

Hockey is played on a rectangle. Five face-off circles are painted onto the ice.

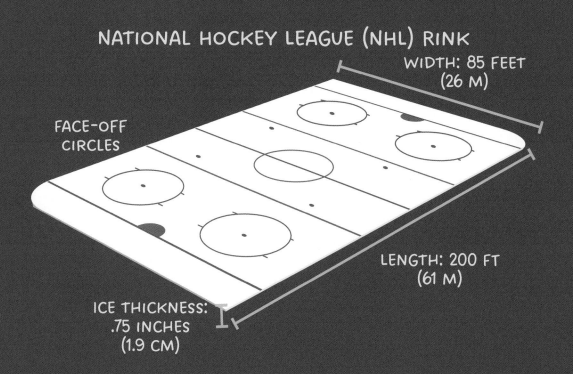

NATIONAL HOCKEY LEAGUE (NHL) RINK

WIDTH: 85 FEET (26 M)

FACE-OFF CIRCLES

LENGTH: 200 FT (61 M)

ICE THICKNESS: .75 INCHES (1.9 CM)

The ice on a hockey rink is made of around 64 layers of frozen water. You can calculate the volume of the ice layer using the formula from page 13:

(length x width x depth) x 7.5 = volume

(200 x 85 x 0.0625 FEET) x 7.5 = VOLUME

(1062.5) x 7.5 = 7,968.75 gallons

American Football

FAST FACTS

- American football is one of the few goal-based sports played on a rectangular field that uses a ball that is not a sphere. This ball is called a prolate spheroid.

- The first football was made of an inflated pig bladder. It was thicker in the middle and slightly pointed on the ends. The ball is no longer made of a pig bladder. But footballs still have that original shape. It is easier to throw longer distances than a round ball.

- American football also has a goal. But it is raised off the ground. It is shaped like a blocky letter Y.

Sports Cylinders

A cylinder is a round three-dimensional shape. Cylinders have a top and bottom that are circular. The pole that holds up a football goalpost is a cylinder. Some basketball goals are held up by a cylinder. Items used to play sports can also be cylinder-shaped.

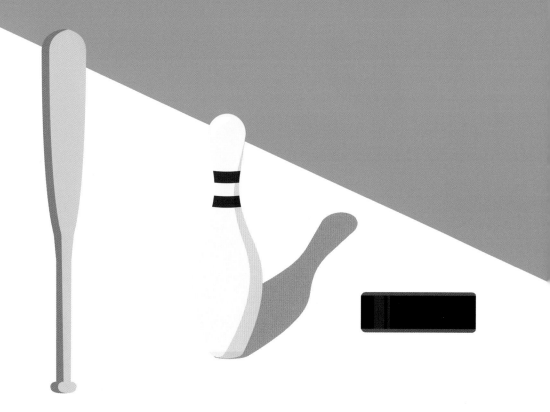

BASEBALL BAT
34 inches (86 cm) x 2.6 inches (6.6 cm)

BOWLING PIN
15 inches (38 cm) x 2 inches (5 cm)

HOCKEY PUCK
1 inch (2.5 cm) x 3 inches (7.6 cm)

Hockey Pucks

The first hockey games ever played used a ball. But a ball on ice is hard to control. Balls bounce and roll, especially on an icy surface. Players found that flat objects worked better. The first modern hockey puck was used in 1940. Pucks are made of hard rubber. They are frozen before games. The frozen rubber cylinder glides smoothly across the ice!

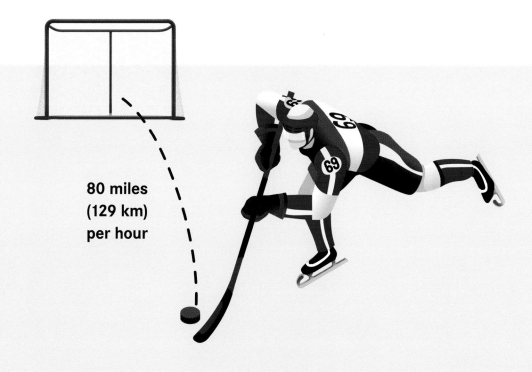

80 miles (129 km) per hour

Average speed of a hockey puck when it is hit: 80 to 100 miles (129 to 161 kilometers) per hour

CHAPTER 3

Shape-Shifting the Game

Like with the hockey puck, sometimes people see a way to make the sport better. Then the rules change. New technology has helped make soccer balls better. Their shape has changed. They are made of better materials. Stadiums have also changed. They come in many sizes and shapes. Some stadiums are for many sports. Others are made for just one sport.

The way athletes play sports has even changed. Coaches have found which formations work best. They have created new formations to make their teams better. New sports with new rules have even been created.

Soccer Balls Through Time

The first soccer balls were not completely spherical. Before rubber was invented, people played soccer with an inflated pig's bladder. It was shaped more like an American football. It did not roll very well. Modern balls have come a long way from a pig's bladder!

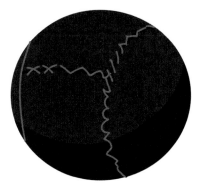

Uruguay, 1930

Brazil, 1950

Chile, 1962

Mexico, 1970

PANATHENAIC STADIUM, 330 BCE

Rectangular with rounded corners; "stadium" is actually the name of a shape. It means a rectangle with rounded ends.

COLISEUM IN ROME, 80 CE

The Coliseum is called the "father of modern stadiums." It has high walls with rows of seating around an oval playing field.

LORD'S CRICKET GROUND, 1812

The first grandstand was built in the early 1800s. Grandstands have long rectangular rows of covered seats. They overlook a cricket or soccer field.

HARVARD STADIUM, 1903

Harvard Stadium is the oldest still-used concrete stadium in the United States. It is shaped like a U or horseshoe.

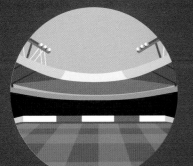

WHITE CITY STADIUM, 1908

The first oval-shaped stadium with seating areas in the curved parts was built in the early 1900s.

ASTRODOME, 1965

The Astrodome was the first fully covered oval-shaped stadium.

SKYDOME TORONTO, 1989

The first retractable roof oval-shaped stadium was built in Canada.

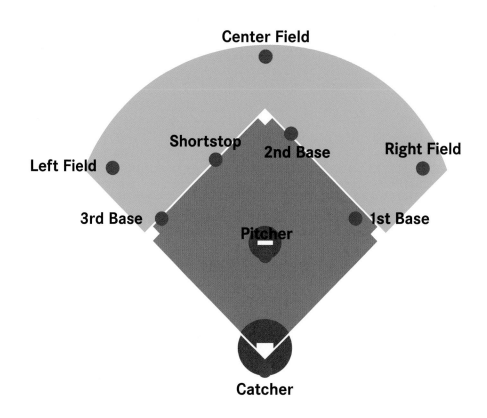

Center Field

Shortstop

2nd Base

Right Field

Left Field

3rd Base

1st Base

Pitcher

Catcher

Shapes on the Field

People create shapes in sports, too. Each player on a team has a position. First, all of the players get into their positions. Then they make a shape called a formation. Some sports have several formations. Others have just one or two. In baseball, the outfield positions are always the same. In soccer, there are many different formations. Soccer coaches might use different formations against a particular team. Or they might change which formation they use to match the skills of the players on their team.

Pickleball vs. Tennis

Pickleball is similar to tennis. It is played on a smaller court with slightly different equipment.

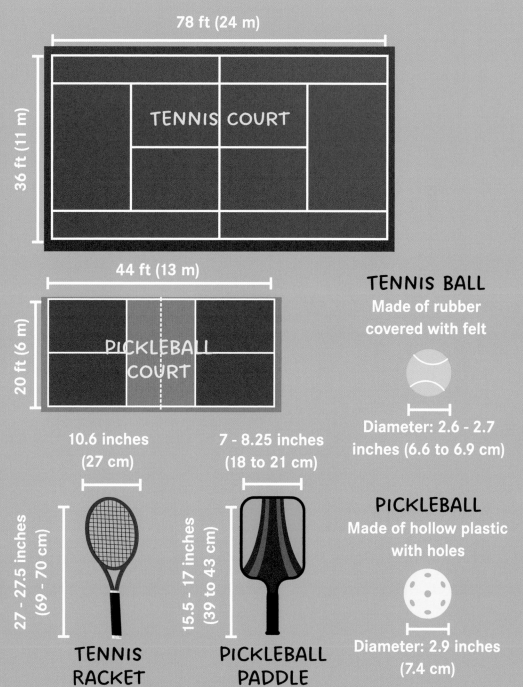

78 ft (24 m)

36 ft (11 m)

TENNIS COURT

44 ft (13 m)

20 ft (6 m)

PICKLEBALL COURT

TENNIS BALL
Made of rubber covered with felt

Diameter: 2.6 - 2.7 inches (6.6 to 6.9 cm)

10.6 inches (27 cm)

7 - 8.25 inches (18 to 21 cm)

27 - 27.5 inches (69 - 70 cm)

15.5 - 17 inches (39 to 43 cm)

TENNIS RACKET

PICKLEBALL PADDLE

PICKLEBALL
Made of hollow plastic with holes

Diameter: 2.9 inches (7.4 cm)

CHAPTER 4

First, Best, Most

Every sport has a first game. The first Olympics took place about 3,000 years ago. The first baseball game was in 1846. Pickleball and snowboarding were invented in the 1960s.

No matter how old or new, every sport has records. Records tell which runner can race around the oval shape of the track the fastest. They list the players who have hit the most spherical balls out of a baseball stadium. Some records are about people who come to stadiums to watch sports. Some are about how big a stadium is or how many balls are used in a game.

FAST FACTS: The First Olympics

The first Olympic Games were in 776 BCE in Olympia, Greece.

There was only one event. It was a foot race around 200 meters (656 feet) long. Racers went from one end of the stadium to the other.

Later, runners eventually ran around the oval stadium. This remained a standard shape in track-and-field events.

A Winning Formation

Real Madrid is considered the most successful professional soccer team in soccer history. It has won 830 games and 94 major cups in the club's long history. One of the club's most used formations is a 4-3-3. This formation has become one of the most used in the sport. It gives teams a strong defensive advantage. It also puts many players in a position to score goals.

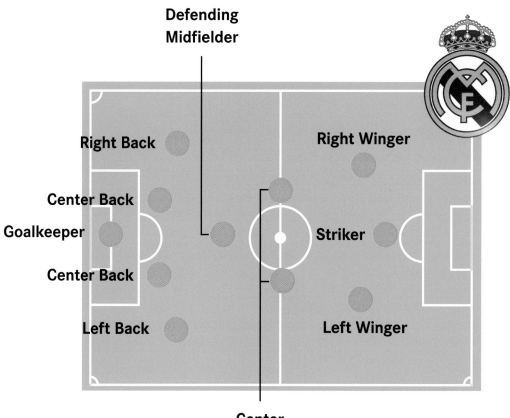

Defending Midfielder

Right Back

Right Winger

Center Back

Goalkeeper

Striker

Center Back

Left Back

Left Winger

Center Midfielder

How Many Balls Does it Take?

Professional sporting events always have plenty of equipment on hand. Players go through a lot of spheres and cylinders during a typical game. By the end of a regular season, the numbers can really add up! Take a look at how many balls and pucks are used in the four major U.S. pro sports leagues.

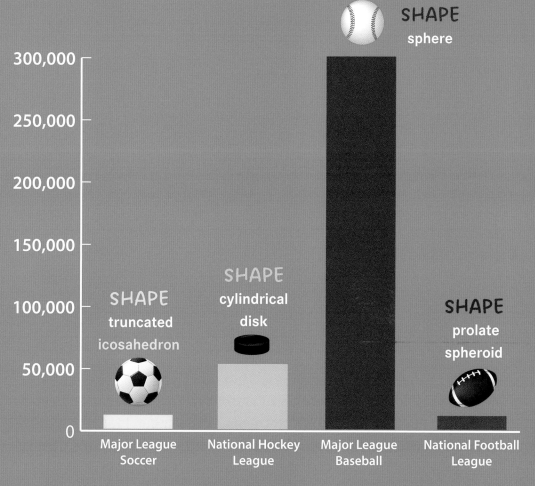

SHAPE
sphere

SHAPE
truncated
icosahedron

SHAPE
cylindrical
disk

SHAPE
prolate
spheroid

300,000

250,000

200,000

150,000

100,000

50,000

0

Major League Soccer

National Hockey League

Major League Baseball

National Football League

2022, Authority Soccer; 2022, NFL World; 2023, DNA of Sports; 2022, Baseball Bible

Unique Shapes and Unusual Locations

HONISTER SLATE MINE
Cumbria, England
World's first underground cricket match, played in 2013 to raise money for a team's flooded cricket grounds; match was played 2,000 feet (610 m) below ground

Rectangular mesh pitch

THE FLOAT
Marina Bay, Singapore
World's largest floating stadium

Rectangle

CARRIER CLASSIC, USS *CARL VINSON*
San Diego, California
First basketball game played on an aircraft carrier between Michigan State and the University of North Carolina, November 11, 2011; standard wooden basketball court was constructed on the carrier's flight deck, which is 252 feet (77 m) wide and has a total area of 4.5 acres (1.8 hectares)

Rectangle

NATIONAL AQUATICS CENTER
Beijing, China
Built for the 2008 Olympics; largest ETFE-covered structure in the world (ETFE is a type of plastic that allows more natural light and heat than glass); 584 x 584 x 102 feet (178 x 178 x 31.1 m)
Three-dimensional rectangular cuboid

RUNGRADO 1ST OF MAY STADIUM
Pyongyang, North Korea
Largest stadium in the world; seats 150,000 people
Circular, shaped like an open parachute

BURJ AL ARAB HELIPAD TENNIS COURT
Dubai, United Arab Emirates
World's highest tennis court; a match was played there between Roger Federer and Andre Agassi in 2005; 1,503 feet (458 m) high
Circle

Activity
Shaping New Rules of the Game

Cricket is one of the few sports with a playing field that can have many different shapes and sizes. But what if you changed the size and shape of a basketball court? A soccer field? What if baseballs were bigger? What if hockey were played with a ball instead of a puck? Pick a sport and make big changes to it by changing the shapes it uses.

Materials Needed:

- **Paper or posterboard**
- **Writing utensils**

1. First, choose a sport. Make sure you understand how the game is already played. This will make it easier to create your own rules.

2. Make a drawing of the field or court. Include the basic equipment used to play.

3. Next, decide what you will change about the playing area. Consider using unique shapes such as triangles and hexagons. Sketch your new field or court.

4. Next, decide what you will change about the equipment. Draw your new equipment.

5. Now, make new rules based on the above changes. Will there be more bases? More goals? Will you need more players?

6. Write a description of your new game. Explain how it is different from the original game. Explain how the original and new shapes are important to how the game is played.

7. Finally, try out your new game! How did your changes affect game play?

Learn More

Books

Hawkes, Chris. *My Encyclopedia of Very Important Sports*. New York: DK Publishing, 2020.

Stark, Kristy. *Fields, Rinks, and Courts: Partitioning Shapes*. Huntington Beach, CA: Teacher Created Materials, 2018.

Online Resources to Explore with an Adult

Kiddle: Sport Facts for Kids

Soccer Training Lab: The Ultimate Guide to Soccer Formations

YouTube: "Geometric Shapes [Science of NFL Football]"

Bibliography

Dimensions. "Sports Equipment."

Dimensions. "Sports Fields."

Schrag, Miles. *The Sports Rules Book*. Champaign, IL: Human Kinetics, 2019.

Glossary

area (AIR-ee-uh) the amount of space inside of a flat shape

boundaries (BAUN-drees) things that show where one area ends and another area begins

bowl (BOHL) in sports, to roll a ball toward a target

cylinder (SILL-uhn-duhr) a shape with straight sides and two circular ends, like a tube

diameter (dye-AM-uh-tuhr) the length between two opposite points of a circle

dimensions (duh-MEN-shuhns) the measurements of a shape or object, such as length and width

formations (for-MAY-shuns) in sports, the ways that players are arranged on courts or fields

icosahedron (ay-kow-suh-HEE-druhn) a ball-like shape with 20 sides

imperial system (em-PEER-ee-uhl SIS-tum) system of measurement that is based on everyday objects and activities

inflated (in-FLAY-ted) filled with air and expanded

metric system (MEH-trik SIS-tim) system of measurement based on units of 10

outfield (OUT-feeld) the area past the central playing space

position (puh-ZIH-shuhn) in sports, the job a player has on a team

radius (RAY-dee-us) a line from the center to the outer edge of a circle

rectangular cuboid (rek-TAYNG-yoo-lur KYOO-boyd) three-dimensional shape that has 6 rectangular sides, 12 edges, and 8 right angles

three-dimensional (three-duh-MEN-shuh-nuhl) a shape or space that has height, length, and depth

Index